SHABBAT
A PEACEFUL ISLAND

"Family at the Sabbath Table"
by Nahum Tschacbasov, New York, 1946

a JEWISH HOLIDAYS book

shabbat
A peaceful island

by Malka Drucker
drawings by Brom Hoban

HOLIDAY HOUSE · NEW YORK

OTHER JEWISH HOLIDAYS BOOKS
Hanukkah: Eight Nights, Eight Lights
Passover: A Season of Freedom
Rosh Hashanah and Yom Kippur: Sweet Beginnings
Sukkot: A Time to Rejoice

Copyright © 1983 by Malka Drucker
All rights reserved
Printed in the United States of America
First Edition

Library of Congress Cataloging in Publication Data

Drucker, Malka.
    Shabbat: a peaceful island.

    (A Jewish holidays book)
    Summary: Discusses the origins, rituals, and
evening meal of the Sabbath holiday; special Sabbaths
that occur during the year; and Sabbath customs
celebrated in other countries. Includes games, recipes,
puzzles, and crafts.
    1. Sabbath—Juvenile literature. [1. Sabbath]
I. Hoban, Brom, ill. II. Title. III. Series.
BM685.D78   1983   296.4'1   83-7900
ISBN 0-8234-0500-1

For Rabbi Harold M. Schulweis,
whose light has warmed me

ACKNOWLEDGMENTS

The author would like to thank the following people for helping with the manuscript: Vicky Kelman, Rabbi Harold M. Schulweis, and especially Sue Alexander, for being a dear friend and nudzhge about this book.

She would also like to thank:

Farrar, Straus & Giroux, Inc., for granting permission to reprint a sentence from *The Sabbath* by Abraham Joshua Heschel. Text copyright © 1975 by Abraham Joshua Heschel.

The Jewish Publication Society of America for permission to reprint Torah portions from the JPS Torah.

CONTENTS

TO THE READER

I've wanted to write this book for a long time because *Shabbat* gave me my introduction to the mystery and drama of Judaism. When I was very young I never saw anyone light candles on Friday night; I never even heard anyone talk about it. I only knew about the ceremony from hearing my Hebrew school teachers describe it. Since lighting candles was no part of my life, I thought it must be an ancient practice, like animal sacrifice, that was no longer done.

One Friday evening a friend invited me to her home for dinner. As I walked into the house, a rich fragrance of fresh-baked bread and chicken soup greeted me. "Have they prepared such a dinner just for me?" I wondered. When we entered the dining room, I saw a beautifully set table. In the center of the table two sturdy white candles gently burned in a pair of shiny brass candlesticks.

As I puzzled about all this, the word *Shabbos* popped into my mind. Instantly I knew that the candles were lit for the Sabbath. To my surprise, Shabbat still existed. Then I realized that the elegance of the evening was not for my benefit but to celebrate the Sabbath that I had been invited to share with my friend. I had a wonderful Shabbat dinner, and I've carried the memory of it ever since.

When I grew up, I wanted to celebrate Shabbat. I found an old pair of candlesticks in my mother's house that had been my great-grandmother's. My grandmother remembered polishing them for her mother, but she never lit them herself. They remained in the family as a memento, but they were tarnished and their purpose had been forgotten.

I took the candlesticks home and polished them until their dull surface, worn smooth by time, became the texture and color of light, shining gold. The first Friday night when I lit and blessed the candles, I felt awkward—I had never seen it done. I mumbled the prayer and wondered where to put the burnt match. But after a while the ritual became familiar and an experience to look forward to. I came to love the ceremony not only for its meaning but for its helping me to feel close to my great-grandmother, although I'd never known her. Those candlesticks also helped me to find my place among the Jewish people.

I hope this book will be like the candlesticks, bringing the reader closer to a precious day and to the people who celebrate it.

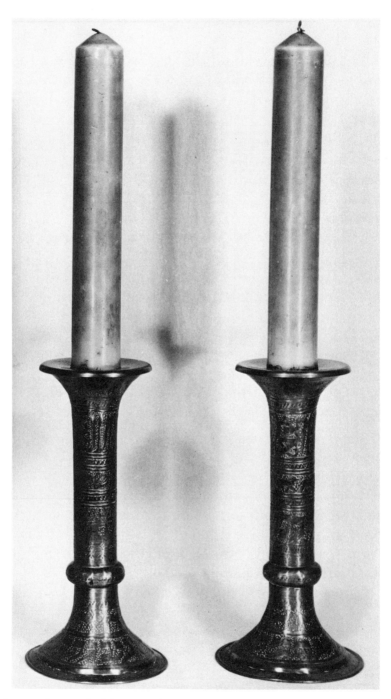

Syrian brass Shabbat candlesticks

1
Light

Let there be light.

GENESIS 1:3

Shabbat, the weekly Jewish day of rest, is supposed to begin at sundown on Friday, but it really begins earlier. Preparing for it ahead of time is also part of the holiday, and the work starts early on Friday. Even if people go to school or work on that day, they try to get home early to get everything ready for Shabbat. Because this work of preparation includes the entire family, everyone helps to bring the mood of the holiday into the home.

Shabbat is a day of rest, but the day before it is the opposite. It is filled with things to do that seem to take up every minute. First, the house must be sparkling clean, because Shabbat is like an honored guest. The house must look as though someone special is coming to visit.

A wonderful dinner is also part of the Shabbat cele-

Two hallot are blessed
on Friday night.
STEPHANIE SABAR

bration. It may be the one meal of the week that the whole family eats together. This meal also takes time to prepare, and if you're lucky enough to have a home-baked *hallah,* the delicious Sabbath bread, it must be mixed and kneaded Thursday night or early on Friday morning. Some people follow the advice of *Shammai,* a great teacher who lived two thousand years ago, and save any special food they have just for Shabbat.

By the late afternoon, after the food is prepared and the table is set, you've begun to get yourself ready for Shabbat. You've bathed and dressed in clothes that are a little fancier than what you wear the rest of the week. If you've bought new clothes, the Sabbath is the time to wear them. Some people play Israeli or Jewish records to fill the house with music which is different from that of the rest of the week. Baking hallah gives the house a special fragrance, too. As the day's light begins to dim, it's time for everyone to breathe a sigh of relief and to look forward to stepping into the warmth and well-deserved peace of the holiday.

Two thousand years ago in Jerusalem, Shabbat was on every Jew's mind all week. Many people didn't work on Friday in order to prepare for the Sabbath. Unlike the present, when stopping one's busy life for a day requires a real effort, in ancient times Shabbat was the reason for all the other days. In fact, the other days of the week had no name. They were simply called the first day to Shabbat, the second day to Shabbat, and so on. Only Shabbat had a name. In the late afternoon, everyone in Jerusalem would listen for six clear, high-pitched notes which were blown from a *shofar,* a trumpet made from a ram's horn. This was the signal to stop working. Farmers left their fields, storekeepers closed their shops, and housewives wrapped with straw the pots in which their Sabbath meals were cooking in order to keep the food hot. Once the Sabbath began, no one was allowed to cook, because it was work.

Although the purpose of Shabbat remained the same throughout Jewish history, different generations added their own ideas to it. The *Kabbalists* in *Safed,* a city in Israel, studied their traditions to find deeper meanings. The Kabbalists thought Shabbat was a way for each person to be close to God and to find God within. On Friday afternoon they went into the fields outside Safed to greet the Sabbath as though the day were a *kalleh,* or bride.

This shofar is similar to the ones used
in ancient Israel to announce Shabbat.
HEBREW UNION COLLEGE SKIRBALL MUSEUM

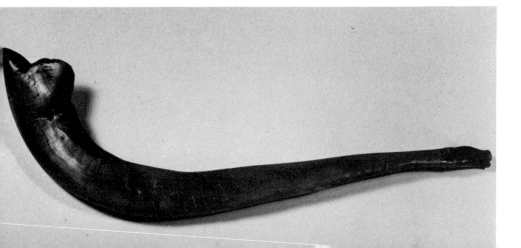

They imagined "their" bride descending on the rays of the setting sun to meet her groom. They dressed in their finest clothes, recited psalms, and sang *"Lekhah Dodi,"* "Come my love, to greet the Sabbath Bride." They called Shabbat a bride because the relationship between a bride and groom expressed their feeling for Shabbat. A groom loves his bride, anticipates her arrival with joy, and wants to embrace her. The Jewish people were Shabbat's lover. The rabbis explained how this worked. Sunday has Monday, Tuesday has Wednesday, Thursday has Friday, but who has Shabbat? The Jewish people have Shabbat. The Sabbath was also called *Shabbat ha-Malkah,* the Sabbath Queen, as a reminder that the laws of the day must be obeyed.

Welcoming the Sabbath Bride became part of the Shabbat celebration and is called the *Kabbalat Shabbat* service. In Eastern Europe one hundred fifty years ago, before the Kabbalat Shabbat, every adult bathed in a *mikveh,* which was a public bath house. Men and women separately immersed themselves in fresh spring water and said appropriate blessings. Their washing symbolized a fresh start or a new life. The week, with its seven days, represented the cycle of creation. Then they dressed in their Sabbath clothes. The men wore black robes tied with a silk belt and a velvet *kippah,* or head covering. Before they rushed to the synagogue to welcome the Sabbath, they carefully emptied their pockets of coins, because you don't carry money on Shabbat. The women dressed in black silk dresses that were brightened by a string of pearls, and welcomed the Sabbath at home. It was the woman's responsibility to light the Sabbath candles eighteen minutes before sundown.

Shabbat in modern America has changed to fit the times, but it is no less powerful or necessary. In some ways resting for one day a week in a society that values work so much may be more important than ever.

Just as in ancient times, Shabbat begins with the setting of the sun. All Jewish holidays begin at sundown because the world began in darkness. The creation of the world is remembered with the lighting of the Shabbat candles, that have to be lit before sunset so that they're kindled in time for the Sabbath. But just before they are lit and everyone can enjoy Shabbat, some money is set aside for the poor. Some people have a little container, called a *pushke,* set beside the Shabbat candles. They put coins into it before blessing the candles.

This girl is holding a pushke that has the word *tzedakah* written on it.   BILL ARON

In Eastern Europe a messenger went to each house in the village with a sack. Some families put money into the sack and some took it out. No one knew who gave and who took. *Tzedakah,* giving to those in need, is a *mitzvah,* a commandment. Giving anonymously is the best kind of tzedakah.

The candles are lit before the holiday for a few reasons. First, you may not light a fire on Shabbat, so if you light the candles beforehand, the house won't be dark for the Sabbath. Secondly, lighting candles separates Shabbat from the workdays. However, some rabbis believed it wasn't necessary to light candles on Shabbat because the light of Shabbat was enough.

The candles are lit eighteen minutes before sundown because eighteen is a special number in the Jewish tradition. Every letter in Hebrew has a numerical equivalent. In ancient times the Jews did not use separate characters for numbers. The letters were used to make words, and they were also used as numbers. Every word, therefore, equaled the numerical sum of its letters. Eighteen is the sum of the letters in the word *chai,* which means "life" in Hebrew.

Custom calls for a woman to light the candles, but they can be lit by anyone. Usually there are two candles lit because there are two versions of the commandment to keep the Sabbath in the Bible: "Remember the Sabbath day" (Exodus 20:8) and "Observe the Sabbath day" (Deuteronomy 5:12). Another more practical reason is because in ancient days, few families lived in more than two rooms. Two candles provided a light for each room during Shabbat.

The two candles also represent the opposites in life:

light and darkness, holy and profane, work and rest. On
Shabbat everything is oneness and harmony. The holiday helps to make the change from time being broken
up into many tasks to time becoming a period of whole-
ness and completion. A person may also feel separated
from others at the start of Shabbat. His concerns and in-
terests may isolate him from the other members of the
family. The Sabbath brings everyone closer together.
Some families light a candle for every member of the
family. In the Middle Ages, wealthy families lowered a
seven-branched candelabrum from the ceiling for Shabbat and lit its candles.

The woman covers her head with a scarf before she
lights the candles. Then she lights the candles and covers
her eyes with her hands. The reason her eyes are covered is a little confusing. She must light the candles before the blessing because once the prayer is said, Shabbat begins and the candles may no longer be lit. But all
blessings must be said *before* a mitzvah is performed, so
she has to cover her eyes in order not to see the candles
already lit. She makes three circular motions with her
hands over the candles as though to bring the Shabbat
lights into her. She puts her hands in front of her eyes
and recites the blessing: "Praised are You, O Lord our
God, King of the Universe, Who has sanctified our lives
through His commandments, commanding us to kindle
the Sabbath lights." She can also add a prayer of her
own like this one: "Blessed be the One Who brings light
to the world and to the Sabbath. May God bless us and
our Sabbath." Sometimes a prayer is so private she
might simply say the words to herself. Afterwards, she
might look at the clear, peaceful flame of the candles.

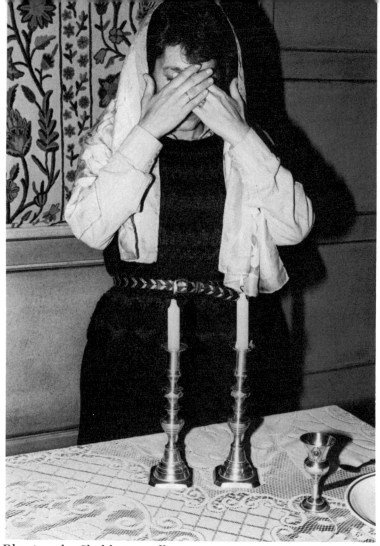

Blessing the Shabbat candles   STEPHANIE SABAR

This is the moment for her to think about the past week, take a deep breath, and feel the mood of Shabbat take over.

Lighting candles is the beginning of the Sabbath, and it is good if the whole family can share it and say the blessings together. Once the candles are lit, they burn until they go out. Nothing is interfered with on Shabbat, including the candles.

Lighting the Shabbat candles was a special problem for the *Marranos*, Jews who secretly practiced their Judaism during the Spanish Inquisition in the fifteenth century. Since they couldn't blow the candles out if they heard somone coming, they invented what they called "God's Light." This was a specially prepared wooden stick in a container of olive oil that was placed in an uncovered jar and lit. When the Marranos sensed danger, they quickly hid the jar, with the flame inside.

There is a short synagogue service that welcomes the Shabbat. It is a form of the Kabbalat Shabbat. Besides "Lekhah Dodi," seven psalms are sung, one for each day of the week. The daily prayer, the *Amidah*, is also said, and it contains seven blessings. The first and the last three are the daily blessings; the middle three are blessings that celebrate Shabbat. The service ends with *Kiddush*, the prayer said over wine that announces the holi-

Three Kiddush cups: French, 19th century;
German, 18th century; American, 1972
HEBREW UNION COLLEGE SKIRBALL MUSEUM

ness of Shabbat. Some synagogues schedule this service to follow dinner at home.

The Friday-night service is an important part of Shabbat, but the day's focus is on the family. This is because the family is the key to the survival of the Jewish people. Jewish life enriches the family, and the family helps to preserve Judaism. Home really is the school for future generations. More than just teaching history and laws, it binds its members to traditions through songs, food, and love. Shabbat may be the one experience the family shares together. School, work, and worries are left behind; Shabbat is a time of pleasure that comes from a family celebration. The family's change of mood is so dramatic that children may think they have four parents—the two weekday parents, who are sometimes tense and short-tempered, and the two Shabbat parents, who are cheerful and relaxed.

There is a *midrash* or legend that describes how everyone who goes to synagogue is followed home by two angels, a good one and a bad one. When people enter their house and it is ready for Shabbat, with the candles lit and the table set beautifully for the dinner, the good angel says, "May it be this way next week." If the house looks no different from any other day of the week, the bad angel says the same thing. This legend is a reminder that Shabbat not only changes people but the house itself. You don't have to leave home to be refreshed and renewed.

If the family goes to the synagogue before dinner, the first thing they do when they arrive home is the *Birkhat ha-Banim*, the Blessing of the Children. The parents place their hands upon the child's head and say: "May

19th-century German lithograph which shows parents saying the Birkhat ha-Banim. THE JEWISH MUSEUM/EDITORIAL PHOTOCOLOR ARCHIVES

God bless you and keep you. May God watch over you in kindness. May God grant you a life of good health, joy, and peace." If the family has not gone to the synagogue, this blessing takes place after lighting the candles.

One of the best parts of Shabbat is the *zemirot,* or songs sung to welcome the Sabbath. They can be sung before, during, and after dinner. *"Shalom Aleichem,"* "Peace Be with You," is a song that welcomes the angels of peace. Its gentle, sweet melody makes it a fine song to sing before the Kiddush at home.

Some people take a wine goblet in one hand, slip the stem of the wine goblet between two fingers and hold

the cup in their palm with their fingers curled upward.
Their hand is shaped like a rose, which is a symbol of
perfection. The Kiddush is usually said over wine, but if
there is no wine, it can be said over the hallah. Everyone
lifts a cup of wine, which is almost brimming over, to
express the overflowing joy of Shabbat, and says:

There was evening and there was morning, the sixth
day. The heavens and the earth, and all they contain,
were completed. On the seventh day God finished the
work which He had been doing; He ceased on the seventh day from all the work which He had done. Then
God blessed the seventh day and called it holy, because
on it He ceased from all His work of creation.

Praised are You, Lord our God, Ruler of the Universe,
Who creates the fruit of the vine.

Praised are You, Lord our God, King of the Universe,
Who has sanctified us through His commandments and
has been pleased with us. You have lovingly and gladly
granted us Your holy Sabbath, recalling the creation of
the world. The Sabbath is first among the days of sacred
assembly which recall the Exodus from Egypt. You have
chosen us, sanctifying us among all people by granting
us Your holy Sabbath lovingly and gladly. Praised are
You, Lord, Who sanctifies the Sabbath.

This prayer, which is sung in Hebrew, thanks God for
the great delight of the Sabbath, for the creation of the
world, and for freeing the Jews from slavery in Egypt.
Both the creation and the Exodus from Egypt are mentioned in the Kiddush because these events are central
to the life of the Jewish people.

Some families wash their hands before they sit down to eat the Shabbat meal. This is not done for cleanliness, since everybody has bathed before dressing. It's done as a reminder of the priests in the Temple who washed before eating. Like the mikveh, the water signifies a new beginning. The world began with water. A bowl of water and a towel are passed around the table, and everyone says: "Praised are You, Lord our God, King of the Universe, Who has sanctified us through His commandments, and commanded us to wash our hands."

Ha-motzi, the blessing over the hallah, follows this ceremony: "Praised are You, Lord our God, King of the Universe, Who brings forth bread from the earth." After the blessing, the hallah is broken into little pieces and passed around the table for everyone to have a taste. Two loaves of bread are blessed to express the feeling of abundance on Shabbat. The hallah isn't cut, because knives shouldn't be part of a ceremony that celebrates love. During the Kiddush, the hallah is covered with a pretty cloth. The cloth is removed when the hallah is blessed. The rabbis said that the hallah is covered to spare its feelings in being blessed after the wine.

There is a story that tells of a rich merchant who wanted to impress his rabbi with how religious he was. He invited the rabbi to his house on Friday night. When it came time to bless the hallah, the merchant's wife forgot to remove the cloth. The husband yelled at his wife for making such a stupid mistake. The rabbi interrupted and said, "The hallah is covered to spare its feelings. If this is done for a loaf of bread, imagine how much more important it is to spare your wife's feelings!" This story is also a reminder that it is the day, not the objects, that is holy. And it is the people who bless these objects—as God blessed the seventh day and made it holy—who give meaning to them.

The Shabbat table is set with a white cloth to radiate the inner light of Shabbat. Many people, especially in Israel, have flowers on the table to add to the sweetness and beauty of Shabbat. Besides the special meal and songs that brighten the evening, the talk at dinner is different from ordinary conversation. The evening is like being around a campfire, where all the people sit close to one another and share ideas with people they know well. They might discuss what happened during the week or in school, but it's not a time for complaining or arguing. It's a time to remember something that occurred in the past week and to talk about it.

Torah means "teaching." Any new experience that teaches you or changes you is Torah. So discussions ranging from world events to the fun of finding a sala-

A family around the Shabbat table   STEPHANIE SABAR

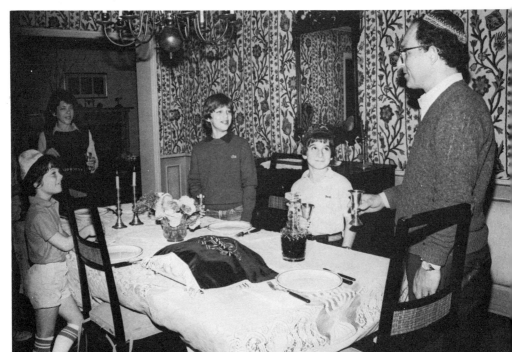

mander on the way to school, or the excitement of making a new friend, are all appropriate for Shabbat.

The dinner, which is leisurely, ends with the *Birkhat
ha-Mazon,* the blessing after the meal:

> Praised are You, Lord our God, King of the Universe,
> Who sustains the whole world with kindness and com-
> passion. He provides food for every creature, for His
> love endures forever. His great goodness has never failed
> us. His great glory assures us nourishment. All life is His
> creation and He is good to all, providing every creature
> with food and sustenance. Praised are You, Lord, Who
> sustains all life.

2

₵ʜє GRєα₵ ꝺαʏ

The Holy One, blessed be He, said unto Moses, "I have a precious gift in my treasure house, and Sabbath is its name. I wish to present it to Israel. Go and bring them the good tidings."

TALMUD

For many Jews, Friday night is a lovely experience that passes too quickly. But Saturday is something else. How will they spend a full day away from the things that keep them busy all week long? It's difficult to shift from busyness to stillness.

Shabbat is not to be spent lying around; *menuhah*, or Shabbat rest, is special. The *Talmud*, which is a collection of commentaries on the Bible that were written by the rabbis fifteen hundred years ago, says Shabbat should be celebrated "with prayer and study, with good food and drink, with clean and becoming clothes, with rest and joy".

Israeli synagogue on Shabbat morning

Prayer and study take place in the synagogue on Saturday morning. This is not like school, however, where you learn new things every day. The rabbis said that on Shabbat you read and study what you've already learned; you bring your own creativity and thoughts to your studies. This is the difference between being smart and being wise.

Shabbat was responsible for the creation of the synagogue. It began with Shabbat gatherings in a Jewish community. Everyone went to the most learned man's house to discuss the weekly portion of the Torah. A different part of the Torah was read three times a week, on Monday, Thursday, and Saturday. On Saturday there was time to discuss that day's portion. The custom of the Shabbat meeting led to holding the Sabbath service and the discussion of the Torah in a house of prayer.

Shabbat was also responsible for creating a love of learning and widespread reading among Jews. Poor and rich people, not just rabbis and scholars, met each week in the synagogue to hear the Torah.

The Saturday-morning service in the synagogue is longer than the daily morning service. In addition to the Torah reading and discussion, more psalms are sung. Because Shabbat is the best day of the week, the Shabbat service is a wonderful time for ceremonies such as the *Bar Mitzvah* (for boys) and the *Bat Mitzvah* (for girls), the coming-of-age celebration for thirteen-year-olds. Babies are given their Hebrew names during the Shabbat morning service, and brides and grooms are called up to the Torah for special honors. The service usually takes three hours, from nine to twelve.

Everyone in the synagogue wears a head covering, usually a kippah, and a *tallit*. The head is covered out of respect for God. The tallit is a large prayer shawl worn over the shoulders. Each of its four corners is fringed with *tzitzit*, which are strings tied into an intricate pattern of knots. Tzitzit are a reminder to obey the laws of

A thirteen-year-old at his Bar Mitzvah ceremony

STEPHANIE SABAR

This man is wearing a tallit. Two of the four tzitzit
can be seen hanging down in front.   IRVING I. HERZBERG

the Torah, and they also represent the four corners of the earth. The laws cover everything in the universe. When the tallit is put on, it creates a private space by enfolding and holding the wearer. When a person becomes a Bar or Bat Mitzvah, he or she is given a tallit to use for life. Eventually the person is buried in it.

Although the service is long, it's not boring. It goes from serious moments of prayer to lively discussions about what the Torah portion means. If a Bar or Bat Mitzvah takes place, there is an added happiness shared by the congregation. After the boy or girl finishes reading a portion of the Torah, a congregation may burst into a lively song to congratulate him or her. Some congregations shower the Bar or Bat Mitzvah with sweetness by throwing candy at him or her. The children at the service madly scramble up to the *bimah*, the platform where the rabbi, *cantor*, and Bar or Bat Mitzvah stand. The children grab all the candy that has fallen.

Before this excitement, the Torah has been carefully covered and carried around the congregation for everyone to kiss. This is done by touching the Torah with one of the tzitzit and then kissing the fringe. Some people touch the prayer book to the Torah and kiss the book. Carrying the Torah is a great honor, but it's not easy. The Torah is not a book as we know it, but a large scroll of parchment rolled around two spools. It is handwritten very carefully by a *sofer*, or scribe, and takes a long time to complete. It weighs at least fifty pounds. After it has circled the congregation, it is brought up to the *aron ha-kodesh*, the holy ark. The doors are opened as the person carrying the Torah stands in front of it. The congregation sings a blessing that includes these words: "It is a tree of life to them that hold fast to it." In some ways, this is a sad moment, because the Torah is being put away. It won't be read with as much leisure and sweetness for another week.

After the service, the congregation may go into another room for a kiddush. Besides wine and hallah, there are often cookies and cake. This snack is called the *Oneg Shabbat,* or Delight of the Sabbath. The congregation goes home where they say another Kiddush and have a hearty lunch, the second meal of Shabbat. The first meal was the Friday-night dinner. (Because breakfast is usually small, it doesn't count as a meal.) Families that do not cook on Shabbat eat a stew that has been cooking since the afternoon before. It's called *cholent,* and it is cooked at a very low temperature. By lunchtime, the chunks of beef mixed with carrots and other vegetables are soft enough to melt in your mouth.

After lunch, many adults feel the need for a nap, but most children are glad to change out of their Shabbat clothes and play games with their friends. The games can be noisy and active, but preferably noncompetitive. Shabbat is not a day to try to beat someone and be the winner.

Once the parents awaken, the family may go visiting, or they may stay home and read stories. There are no special tales that have to be read, but stories with the theme of creation and freedom belong to the day. The story about Noah and the flood is especially good because it tells of a time when the creation was threatened. God was unhappy with human beings. They didn't value the world He had made. He felt that the only way the world could go on was if He destroyed every living

"The Sabbath Afternoon" by Moritz Oppenheim,
Germany, 1866   HEBREW UNION COLLEGE SKIRBALL MUSEUM

thing except Noah and his family, and a male and female
of each species of animal. He told Noah to build a great
ark or boat and take his family and animals into it. Noah
did, and after all the animals and people were on board,
it rained for forty days and forty nights. The world was
entirely flooded. Perhaps because all the living creatures
in the ark knew that their survival was essential to the
world's, they didn't fight or hurt one another. When the
rains stopped, a rainbow appeared. God thought about
what He had done and made a promise. He would never
destroy the world again by flooding it and told Noah
that the rainbow would be a sign of this promise.

The rabbis wrote that God realized also that He had misunderstood the nature of people. Until the flood, human beings were not allowed to kill for food. They were only allowed to eat plants. After the flood, He told Noah that human beings would be allowed to hunt, but they must be compassionate when they killed animals that they ate. For example, they must not cut a limb off a living animal and eat it, but must kill the animal first. Noah's story shows how important it is to live together

Noah sends a dove to find dry land after the flood.
ALINARI/EDITORIAL PHOTOCOLOR ARCHIVES

peacefully and to be careful not to do anything that might destroy creation. It also shows that no object, even the life-giving water from which the world began, is holy. After all, the same water nearly destroyed the world. There are no special objects that must be used on Shabbat. Only the day is holy, because God sanctified it. For six days, He created the things of the world, but on the seventh day, He created the soul, or spirit. This can't be seen, but it can be found inside everyone. The seventh day "re-souls" the world. Human beings, made in God's image, have the power, through their good deeds, to preserve and repair the world.

Some families go out for a walk and go to a park, a stream, or a beach. They may visit these places on other days, but on Shabbat they may seem different. The natural world's link to creation becomes stronger. To appreciate its beauty and its place in the universe is a mitzvah.

Before the Sabbath ends, the family returns home to eat the third meal of the holiday. This meal is not quite as happy as the other two meals, because the sun is beginning to set, a reminder that Shabbat will soon be over. Three meals are eaten, because the custom in ancient times was to eat only two meals on workdays. Three meals set Shabbat apart from the rest of the week. This third meal, called *se'udah shelishit,* is eaten in the late afternoon and is often just a snack or a leftover dessert from lunch.

Some people find it difficult to celebrate Shabbat and keep its laws. Either they feel they must work, or they don't feel ready to devote one-seventh of their lives to dropping out of the busy modern world and stepping into a day of rest. They may also feel they don't know enough to celebrate Shabbat. But Shabbat is called a day of delight, and it's not a day to feel guilty or ignorant. If a person wants to taste the sweetness of the day, he or she can begin slowly, by beginning with one act, such as lighting the candles, and adding a little more as he or she learns and feels ready for it.

Havdalah ceremony   BILL ARON

3
THREE STARS

More than the Jews have kept the Sabbath,
the Sabbath has kept the Jewish people.

AHAD HA-AM (1856–1927), Israeli essayist

Even though Shabbat begins at sundown it doesn't end at sundown. It ends at nightfall, which was defined by the rabbis as the time when three stars appear in the sky. By ending at nightfall, the Sabbath does not end too soon and lasts beyond dusk. Three stars appear roughly forty minutes after sunset. The ceremony to mark the conclusion of the day is called *Havdalah*, which means "separation" in Hebrew. Just as it is difficult to leave one's routine to celebrate Shabbat, it takes an effort to leave Shabbat and return to the ordinary days of the week. The Havdalah helps to make the transition.

Ending the Sabbath is a little like beginning the Sabbath. You light a special candle, bless the wine, and sing songs. But there are important differences. First, the

candle is unusual. It must be one candle with at least
two wicks, and is often four thin candles woven into a
single torch. At the start of Shabbat there are two separate candles. The Havdalah candle is like the coming together of the Shabbat candles. It is a sign of the harmony
created by Shabbat. The light of the candle is different
from the Shabbat candles, too. The candles on Friday
night burn peacefully and quietly, but the Havdalah
candle burns brightly, almost wildly. It is the fire of
creation, the inner fire to give you strength to work in
the world..

19th-century Havdalah
candle in a special
brass candlestick
THE JEWISH MUSEUM/EDITOR-
IAL PHOTOCOLOR ARCHIVES

Besides taking place in a synagogue, the ceremony can be held outside under the stars, or in a house. If it does take place in a house, the lights should be off. The candle is held, usually by a child, while the Havdalah prayers are said. The candle is held high so that the holder will marry a tall bride or groom. The wine cup is filled to the brim to symbolize a full week, and everyone says: "Praised are You, Lord our God, King of the Universe, Who creates the fruit of the wine." No one drinks the wine yet.

Because this is a wistful time, everybody at the Havdalah ceremony needs something extra to help say good-bye to Shabbat. Rabbi Simeon ben Lakish, a teacher who lived in the first century C.E., described a person on Shabbat as having an additional, or higher, soul called *neshamah yeterah.* This soul increases a person's sensitivity to the joy of Shabbat. Everything seems better on Shabbat, even food. At the end of Shabbat, this soul leaves until the next Shabbat. Sweet spices, such as cinnamon and cloves, contained in a little box called the *besamim* box, help to give everyone strength when the neshamah yeterah departs. The fragrance of the spices is a reminder of the sweetness of the holiday. The box may have tiny holes in it to let out the fragrance. Some have playful and charming designs on them such as a windmill or a castle. The spice box is lifted and the following blessing is said: "Praised are You, Lord our God, King of the Universe, Who creates diverse spices." Then the spice box is passed around and everyone sniffs it.

The candle is looked at again and everyone says: "Praised are You, Lord our God, King of the Universe, Who creates the light of fire." At this point each person

Spice box for Havdalah

holds out his or her hands and turns them so that the fingernails face the fire. The light of the fire is reflected in the nails and casts a shadow on the palms. There are a few reasons for this gesture. The simplest is that by using the light to see one's hands, the blessing is said for a purpose. Another reason is that the light on the nails and the darkness of the shadow represent the separation of light and darkness.

The rabbis found a poetic reason for this tradition, too. They explained that when Adam and Eve were in the Garden of Eden, they were covered with the substance of fingernails and toenails. Because of this they were able to stand before the extraordinary radiance of God's light. The nail reflected the light. When Adam and Eve left the Garden of Eden, they lost this protective covering, but a little remained on their fingers and toes. When you hold your hands up to the Havdalah candle on Saturday night, you remember the time when a human being was closer to God and hope for that time again.

The ceremony ends with this prayer said over the wine: "Praised are You, Lord our God, King of the Universe, Who makes a division between the sacred and secular, between light and darkness, between Israel and the other nations, between the seventh day and the six working days. Praised are You, Lord, Who makes a distinction between the sacred and the secular." Then everyone drinks from the Kiddush cup. A little of the wine may be sprinkled on the children present at the Havdalah ceremony to help them grow taller, on a person's eyebrows for wisdom, and on his pockets for wealth. After this, the candle is put out in what is left of the wine.

Many families extend the Havdalah by singing songs, especially about *Elijah*. Elijah was a prophet who is supposed to announce the coming of the Messiah. There are many legends about Elijah's good deeds. One of them tells how every Shabbat, Elijah dresses as a needy stranger and visits Jewish houses. He watches how they greet and welcome him into their homes. The story makes clear that when someone comes to you in need, that stranger could be the prophet Elijah.

Some families prolong Shabbat by having a Saturday-evening meal, called *melavveh malkah*, after Havdalah. This is a good time to tell stories about Elijah or about a certain magical river. Two thousand years ago a tale was told about a wonderful river, *Sambatyon*, that only flowed occasionally. A little community of Jews lived peacefully and securely by it in a distant unknown land. They were supposed to be direct descendants of Moses. The Sambatyon was their protector. For six days it flowed wildly and kept enemies from crossing it. On the seventh day it stopped running, but it sent up a thick fog

17th-century German Havdalah candlestick
HEBREW UNION COLLEGE SKIRBALL MUSEUM

to hide the people. Shabbat protects those who observe it just as the river protected the Jews in the story.

Even though Shabbat actually ends Saturday night, its mood lingers and affects the rest of the week. On Sunday the spirit of Shabbat is still a fresh memory. On Monday the Torah is read and reminds you of Shabbat. On Tuesday night the spirit of Shabbat finally leaves. But on Wednesday the hint of the Shabbat to come appears in the morning psalms. They are part of the Kabbalat Shabbat service. On Thursday the Torah is read, and this helps to set the mood for the coming Shabbat. On Friday there is much work to be done to get ready for Shabbat. At last the day arrives. In this way, a person lives from Shabbat to Shabbat.

4

SPECIAL SABBATHS

*The Sabbath comes like a caress, wiping
away fear, sorrow and somber memories.*

A. J. HESCHEL, *The Sabbath*

Although every Shabbat is special, there are some Sabbaths that are extra-special. In fact, nearly half the Sabbaths celebrate something more than a day of rest. They usually are the Sabbaths before a holiday. They each have their own customs and prayers.

The Shabbat before *Passover* is called *Shabbat ha-Gadol*, the Great Sabbath. On this day the rabbis talk about the laws of Passover. Many years ago this was one of the few times the rabbis spoke to the congregation. Some people think the holiday got its name from the great length of the rabbi's sermon.

The Sabbath before *Rosh Hashanah* is called *Shabbat Shuvah*, the Sabbath of Return. The portion of the *Haftarah*, which is taken from the Prophets, a section of the Bible, is read. It begins, "Return, O Israel, to the Lord thy God" (Hosea 14:1).

Shabbat Bereshit is the Shabbat after *Simhat Torah.* The word *bereshit* means "in the beginning," and it is also the name of the first book of Moses. On that Shabbat the cycle of the Torah reading begins with the first portion of the five books of Moses. It takes a year to read the entire Torah.

Four special Sabbaths occur before Passover, which falls on the fifteenth day of the Hebrew month *Nisan,* and each Sabbath has a special Torah reading. The first is *Shabbat Shekalim.* Its name came from the ancient Jewish community's custom of contributing money, or *shekels,* to the maintenance of the Temple. *Shabbat Zakhor* falls before Purim. *Zakhor* means "remembrance," and on this Shabbat a portion of the Torah is read that commands Jews to remember what Israel's enemies did. *Shabbat Parah* falls two weeks before the month of Nisan, and *Shabbat ha-Hodesh* falls just before the first of Nisan. It is the Sabbath on which Nisan is marked as the first Hebrew month of the year and on which the laws of Passover are described.

Shabbat Shirah is the Sabbath of Song. It is named for the song that Moses and the Israelites sang after they crossed the Red Sea. *Shabbat Hazon* means Sabbath of Vision. It comes before *Tishah be-Av,* the saddest of all Jewish holidays during which Jews mourn the destruction of the Temple. *Shabbat Nahamu* is the Sabbath of Consolation and immediately follows Tishah be-Av.

Besides these Sabbaths, eleven Sabbaths (twelve in a leap year) announce the new moon. Each one of these Sabbaths is called *Shabbat Mevarekhim.* There is a special blessing, called the *Birkhat ha-Hodesh,* that announces the new month and asks God for a month of blessings. In ancient times this announcement was very

20th-century oil painting of the
blessing of the new moon, Anonymous

important, because every new moon begins a new month. The Jewish people needed to know the day of the new month in order to calculate their holidays. For example, the Torah says, "In the first month, on the fourteenth day of the month, at twilight, there shall be a passover offering to the Lord, and on the fifteenth day of that month the Lord's feast of unleavened bread" (Leviticus 23:5–6). The Jews had to know what the first day of the month was in order to predict when the fourteenth and fifteenth days would occur.

How did they determine when the new moon appeared? By their eyes. Two witnesses, often young boys, sat on top of *Mount Moriah* and kept watch for the first glimpse of the new moon. As soon as they saw it, they lit a torch that could be seen throughout Israel. Bonfires would be lit as soon as people could see the first torch. This would happen on the twenty-ninth or thirtieth day of each month.

Shabbat Rosh Hodesh is a Sabbath that falls on the first day of the month, and a special Torah portion (Exodus 12:1–20) and a special Haftarah are read. In addition, the moon itself is blessed in a ceremony called *Birkhat ha-Levanah.* This ceremony can be done any day from the third to the fourteenth day of the month, but many Jews try to do the ceremony after Havdalah to extend the joy of Shabbat.

Birkhat ha-Levanah must be performed outside when the moon can be seen. Prayers are said, songs are sung, and at one point everyone stands on tiptoe to get closer to the moon. Besides being a dramatic and beautiful ceremony, it is also a way to appreciate this natural clock in the sky.

The Jewish people celebrate *Rosh Hodesh,* the monthly holiday of the new moon, because their calendar is based on the moon's cycle. But there is another reason for their blessing the moon. The rabbis said that the Jews are like the moon. The other nations of the world were like the sun, always big and strong, but the Jews were like the ever-changing moon. Sometimes they have been big and strong, like a full moon, but at other times they have been small and weak, like the sliver of a new moon. During the difficult and frightening times, the Jewish people remembered that, like the moon, they would be strong again. The Torah also says that there will be a time when the moon will shine as brightly as the sun.

Reading the Torah on Shabbat morning   BILL ARON

5

REMEMBER
AND OBSERVE

*On Shabbat a man should always walk
with an easy and leisurely gait, but to do a
good act, a man should always run, even
on Shabbat.*

TANHUMA, *Bereshit.*

When you look through a kaleidoscope, you see intricate
shapes and lively colors that form a unique design.
Shabbat is like a kaleidoscopic image of all the Jewish
holidays, each colored facet representing one holiday.
Passover has a special meal, *Shavuot* has the Torah, the
High Holy Days have a mood of joyful seriousness, *Sukkot* has a little dwelling, *Hanukkah* has lights, and *Purim*
has wine and laughter.

Every week the Sabbath gives a taste of the variety of
rituals, moods, and ideas that are celebrated on these
other holidays during the year. But more than this,

Shabbat is a wonderful day by itself. In fact, it has held the Jewish people together for three thousand years.

When did this special day begin? Some people believe that it started at the beginning of the world. God, Who blessed only the last day of His creation, celebrated the first Shabbat. The other six days, without blessing, were ordinary and separate from the seventh day.

The Jewish people began to celebrate Shabbat over three thousand years ago. The first mention of the holiday is in the Torah. It describes how surprised the Israelites were to find *manna*. This was a white edible plant that became the Israelites' survival food in the wilderness. It appeared in the barren desert where nothing grew. They always found enough manna to gather for one day. If they left any over, it spoiled overnight. On the sixth day, however, they found enough manna for two days, so they picked a double portion. No manna appeared the next day. The manna they had picked the day before was still fresh and lasted until Saturday night. From this experience the Israelites learned not to gather food on the seventh day, because it is a "Sabbath to the Lord." The two loaves of hallah on Shabbat are a reminder of the double portion of manna.

Shabbat appears again in the Ten Commandments. The Fourth Commandment (in Exodus) says, "Remember the Sabbath day, and keep it holy. Six days you shall labor and do all your work, but the seventh day is a Sabbath of the Lord your God: you shall not do any work— you, your son, or daughter, your male or female slave, or your cattle, or the stranger that is within your settlements. For in six days the Lord made heaven and earth and sea, and all that is in them, and He rested on the

Linen hallah cover by Sharon Norry, 1981

seventh day; therefore the Lord blessed the Sabbath day and hallowed it" (Exodus 20:8–11). Shabbat is the only holiday mentioned in the Ten Commandments.

What does the word *Shabbat* mean? Its simplest definition is "rest." It comes from the root word meaning "cease and desist." On the seventh day, God *"shavat mi kol melakhto"*: God ceased and desisted from all His work. So the celebration of Shabbat is a way of acknowledging that God created the world. According to some people, Shabbat is also one of God's names. God revealed his name to Moses, but when the Temple was destroyed in Jerusalem two thousand years ago, the Jewish people lost God's name. *God, the Lord, Almighty, King,* and *Ruler of the Universe* are all substitutes for the name and are never said casually or disrespectfully.

That Shabbat is one of those substitute names is another expression of the day's power. By celebrating Shabbat, you imitate God. He rested on the seventh day. You bless the day and affirm the miracle of creation that can be found in every living thing.

Although the Jews were the first people to celebrate a day of rest, they may have gotten the idea from their neighbors, the Babylonians. Four thousand years ago, the Babylonians had a holiday they called *Sapattu.* Every seven days they noticed that the moon went into a different phase. They feared that at such time, their gods would become angry with them if they did something wrong. So during each new phase of the moon, their king, who represented the gods, would do as little as possible on this day they considered unlucky. He wouldn't set a fire, ride in his chariot, or change his clothes. Priests and physicians also observed Sapattu. The Babylonians believed that if they underwent hardship and restrictions, their angry gods would be satisfied.

The Jewish Sabbath, however, had nothing to do with an angry god or the moon. The Jewish people celebrated the seventh day as a time to remember God's creation of the world. They did no work on that day. To separate it further from the Babylonian Sabbath, the Jews began their day of rest with brightly glowing candles. Shabbat was a day filled with light, not gloomy darkness.

Shabbat was also different from the Babylonian Sabbath because not only the priests but the entire Jewish community celebrated the holiday. All Jews were equal in their observance of this day, which was a gift from God. Furthermore, since every living creature is part of the world's creation, all of the Jewish household rested.

Children, servants, guests, and animals enjoyed Shabbat, just as the Fourth Commandment instructed. It wasn't as though a Jewish farmer could slouch in his easy chair on Shabbat while his servants did his work for him.

Besides creation, Shabbat celebrates freedom from slavery. The Fourth Commandment (in Deuteronomy) says, "Remember that you were a slave in the land of Egypt and the Lord your God freed you from there with a mighty hand and an outstretched arm; therefore the Lord your God has commanded you to observe the Sabbath day" (Deuteronomy 5:15). The Jewish people are supposed to remember their own slavery under the Egyptians two thousand years ago so as to be more sen-

Moses leading the Israelites across the Red Sea
to escape slavery in Egypt (The Exodus),
Gutenberg Bible, 15th century
TOWER NEWS SERVICE/EDITORIAL PHOTOCOLOR ARCHIVES

sitive to how they treat other people. Most important, Shabbat reminds the Jews that God rules over the earth. No person, regardless of his power, has that authority. Shabbat is a day when no one is "boss" over anything.

Shabbat set Judaism apart from all other religions. Many peoples were mystified by the Jews' day of rest. The Greeks and Romans thought the Jews were lazy, sometimes letting themselves be killed rather than fight on the Sabbath. After hundreds of Jews were massacred on the Sabbath, Jews realized that not fighting on their day of rest was a mistake. As a result, if one's life is in danger, it is always permissible to break the Sabbath. The Sabbath is to live by, not to die by.

Some of the rabbis believed that Shabbat is the most important law of the Torah and that by itself it is equal to all the rest. They wrote, "If Israel keeps one Sabbath as it should be kept, the Messiah will come." This didn't mean that they would be rewarded by a supernatural savior. It meant that Shabbat is a taste of the world to come, a perfect world. The Jews could experience, one day a week, harmony and peace on earth. The seventh day is the Jewish answer to easing human pain and suffering. An observant Jew believes that Shabbat is as necessary to saving the world as nuclear disarmament is. The greeting on Shabbat is *"Shabbat Shalom,"* which means "May you have a Sabbath of peace."

The question is, however, what exactly does the Fourth Commandment mean? How do you keep Shabbat? What is rest? What is work? Two thousand years ago the rabbis carefully studied the Torah for clues to making the laws of Shabbat clear. This effort also made the meaning of the holiday clear for future generations.

The first hint of how to celebrate Shabbat came in the two versions of the Fourth Commandment. The first time, in Exodus, it says, "Remember (Zakhor) the Sabbath day," and the second time, in Deuteronomy, it says, "Observe (*shamur*) the Sabbath day." The rabbis explained that to *remember* is to know the reason for the Shabbat laws. In other words, to understand the ideas celebrated by the day. *Observe* means to make the ideas real with deeds. You must do something to remember why the holiday is important.

The rabbis described specific rules for what to do and not to do on Shabbat. The laws fell into two categories, negative and positive. The laws of observing were negative, what must not be done on Shabbat, and the laws of remembering were positive, what must be done on Shabbat. The rabbis reasoned that since the laws of Shabbat that were in the Torah immediately followed the laws of building the Tabernacle, the great house of prayer in the desert, acts of construction should be forbidden on the Sabbath. The rabbis therefore divided the tasks for building the Tabernacle into thirty-nine categories. (See Appendix.) These "forbidden acts of the Sabbath" defined what was work. Sowing, reaping, and carrying are a few examples of them. Even though most Jews are not builders or farmers, the laws are important. The idea is to build a day, not a physical dwelling like the Tabernacle. Shabbat has lasted for three thousand years, and few buildings can match its age. Time, not space or matter, is the focus of the holiday. However, any of the laws can be broken to save a life. In Israel, the Sabbath has been broken for national emergencies and military service.

The negative laws keep you from interfering with the physical world, too. By letting the physical world rest for a while, human beings are able to rest, too. Carrying is a good example of this. It's all right to carry things around in your house, but you can't carry things from a private place to a public place. (Sometimes a community, especially in Israel, will build an *eruv*, a fence, around itself so that objects can be transported within its walls.) The point of this law is that you do not try to change the world on Shabbat, even by simply moving an object from one place to another. How does carrying affect the world? Think how different the world would be if no one carried money.

Another reason for the carrying law is more personal. Imagine how good it feels to come home from school and immediately slip off a heavy backpack full of books and papers. It's a great relief to put away the backpack on Friday afternoon and know you are commanded not to even think about its contents until the following evening.

You do not light a fire on Shabbat because the "light" of Shabbat is enough. Fire is also one of the ways human beings can control the environment. Without it people cannot prevail and dominate. The "fire" of anger, envy, and competition should be avoided on the Sabbath. In modern times fire includes electricity, because it is an outside source of energy. It is all right, though, to turn on lights in an oven before sundown. Shabbat is a time to turn inward to discover your inner energies. It is a time to talk to your friends, but not on the telephone. You can listen to yourself and others without the intrusion of an instrument. You can read but not write, because pencil

These children enjoy a rest from schoolwork on Shabbat.
IRVING I. HERZBERG

and paper are another outside source of energy. In Israel, essential electricity is present so that no one has to turn it on during Shabbat. An elevator is set to stop automatically on every floor of an apartment building so that no one has to control where it stops on the Sabbath. All stores are closed, and in Jerusalem there is no public transportation. It's easier to celebrate Shabbat in Israel than anywhere in the world, because almost everyone else is observing it, too. There are fewer temptations— like movies or television—but more than that, the spirit of Shabbat is contagious.

Conservative Jews have modified the laws to allow driving a car to the synagogue or to visit a sick person. Driving to the synagogue is often necessary if you live far away, but if you can avoid whizzing along the road for any reason on Shabbat, it's much better. Walking helps your eyes to "slow down" and see what's around you. During the week there may not be time to stroll along and watch a squirrel contentedly munch an acorn.

Not doing work is only half of Shabbat. The absence of work allows time for the leisurely moments which make the day a delight. Every "no" allows for a "yes." The quiet and stillness of Shabbat give you a chance to appreciate the work you've done all week. There is a legend that describes how precious Shabbat is. God said to the Jewish people, "If you follow My laws and accept the Torah, I will give you the most valuable gift I have, the world to come."

"Show us here an example of this world," the Jews asked. So God gave them Shabbat, which is a taste of the perfect world. They didn't have to die to experience eternity. They could have it every week.

"Friday Night Sabbath" by Isidor Kauffmann, Vienna, ca. 1900

THE JEWISH MUSEUM/EDITORIAL PHOTOCOLOR ARCHIVES

Many Jews who celebrate Shabbat do not observe the day strictly. They may turn on lights or listen to music on the stereo. But they try to keep the point of Shabbat clear. They don't want the day so filled with prohibitions that it becomes a burden rather than a joy. If they play music, it's Israeli or Jewish music to help them get into the mood of Shabbat. If they postpone lighting candles until after dark, it's so that the entire family can be together, to usher in Shabbat. Their focus is on the spirit of the day.

The laws of Shabbat may seem difficult to keep. They may feel restrictive, as they interfere with weekly activities. But many Jews find that the longer they celebrate Shabbat, the less the laws constrain them. Besides freeing them from work, the laws free them from routine, schedules, and boredom. The problem is that it's easy to misunderstand freedom. Some people might want to be free to watch unlimited television. At first they have a great time watching anything they feel like, but after a while, they find themselves watching boring, stupid shows because television has enslaved them. Are they still free not to watch?

The laws of Shabbat build a fence around the day, and the day is like a home that shelters, warms, and comforts people from the setting of the sun on Friday night until three stars appear in a darkening sky the following evening. The more everybody visits this "peaceful island," the more they want to return. The days of the week are the path that leads to its door.

6

chicken soup
and hallah

*A simple vegetable meal on the Sabbath in
a home where there is love among husband, wife, and children is better than a
fatted ox in a home where there is hatred.*

JUDAH HE-HASID, medieval writer

Food is an important part of the Jewish holidays. This is
not simply because it's fun to eat special treats, but because eating is a holy act. It is a mitzvah to eat well on
festivals. Shabbat, which celebrates the world's creation
and the creative energy which gives life to the world,
assures you of at least three delicious meals a week. The
neshamah yeterah makes even ordinary food taste special.

Today many families eat well all week long. The food
on Shabbat may not be so different from what's eaten
the rest of the week. But the preparation for the Shabbat
meals is still an important part of getting ready for the

day. In Eastern Europe a century ago, most Jews lived hard lives with much work and very little money. For them Shabbos food, especially on Friday night, was special. They looked forward to the only meal they might eat all week. No matter how poor they were, they put aside something special for Shabbat. A typical Friday dinner might be chicken soup, *gefulte* (stuffed) fish, roasted chicken, kugel (pudding), and hallah.

Bread was a large part of the European Jew's diet because it was cheap and plentiful. Everyday bread was coarse, chewy, and dark—something like stale pumpernickel bread. By contrast, hallah on Shabbat was as splendidly different as was Shabbat itself from the other days of the week. It was yellow-white, made from precious white flour and eggs, fluffy, and sweet.

Hallah (the word means "dough" in Hebrew) is still a treat, especially home-baked hallah. Besides being a delicious part of the Shabbat dinner, its fragrance while baking helps to set the mood for Shabbat. It's also fun to make the braids that form the shape of the bread. Jewish women began the custom of braiding bread in Germany. German women in the Middle Ages baked braided loaves for *Berchta,* an ancient German goddess of vegetation, and called the bread *berches.*

The first blessing for hallah doesn't begin Friday night but at the time when the dough for the bread is first prepared. After the dough is made, a tiny piece, about the size of an olive, is taken and thrown into the hot oven, and the following blessing is said: "Blessed are You, O Lord our God, King of the Universe, Who has hallowed us by His commandments and commanded us to take of the hallah." This mitzvah of separating and throwing away part of the dough has its roots in Temple times, when part of the hallah was broken off and given to the priests.

HALLAH

1 package of dry yeast
1 cup warm water (98° F.)
1½ teaspoons salt
2 teaspoons sugar
3 eggs
2 teaspoons vegetable oil
3½ cups unbleached white flour (bleached is all
  right if you can't find unbleached)
¼ cup poppy or sesame seeds
¼ cup raisins (optional)

Pour the yeast into a large bowl and mix in the warm water until the yeast is dissolved. Add the salt and sugar and stir until they dissolve. Lightly beat in two of the eggs and oil. Slowly add 3 cups of the flour, stirring it into the liquid as you do.

Sprinkle a large cutting board with the remaining ½ cup of flour, and put the dough on it. Knead the flour by pressing the heel of your hand into the center of the dough and turning your hand to flatten the dough. Then fold the dough in half, and keep kneading it for another five minutes. This will make the hallah springy and light. Put the dough back into the bowl and cover it with a damp cloth to keep the surface from getting dry.

The dough needs at least two hours to rise, so it's a good idea to make it before preparing the rest of the

Shabbat meal. Some people even mix the dough Thursday night and put it in the refrigerator. Then they take the mixture out on Friday morning to rise. You can also make the hallah from scratch first thing on Friday morning.

After the hallah has risen to twice its original size, punch down the dough. Don't forget to tear off a tiny piece for the separation prayer. Knead raisins into the dough if you like. Put the rest of the dough on a lightly floured cutting board and divide it in half. Take one half and divide it into thirds. Take each third and roll it into a long "snake." Line up the "snakes" next to one another and braid them like this:

Take the second half and braid it the same way. Separate the yolk from the white of the third egg and, with your fingers, paint the surface of the hallah with yolk. Sprinkle the loaves with poppy seeds or sesame seeds. Put the loaves on a cookie sheet and bake them in a preheated 350° F. oven for 45 minutes.

This recipe makes two small hallot. But if you're having company, you can double the recipe and braid each hallah more grandly.

After the dough has risen and it's ready for braiding, divide it in half, as before. But instead of dividing each half into three pieces, divide each half into four pieces. Roll three pieces into "snakes" and braid them. Take the fourth piece and divide it into three pieces. This is not as complicated as it sounds. Make three little "snakes" and braid them. Take this tiny hallah and lay it on top of the big hallah. Be sure it's on firmly and won't fall off during the baking. Braid the second half of the dough the same way. Cover the two large hallot with egg yolk and seeds, and bake them for an hour. When the hallot are done, take them out of the oven to cool on a cookie sheet or a wire rack.

Most bread is sliced with a knife, but the custom is not to cut hallah. Shabbat is supposed to be a day of peace, and knives are instruments of war. When the Shabbat meal begins, the bread is broken into pieces with the hands and given to everyone at the table. Another way to distribute the hallah is to have everyone grab a little part of it during the ha-motzi and when it ends to pull off a piece. This can be a frisky thing to do at a peaceful dinner, but it's a perfectly appropriate way to avoid using knives on Shabbat.

Cholent, which is something like beef stew, is a traditional Shabbat food for a few reasons. First of all, it can be prepared on Friday and left to cook for twenty-four hours, so the mitzvah of not cooking on Shabbat can be kept without having to forgo a hot meal Shabbat afternoon. In ancient times the ingredients were put in a large pot, brought to a boil, and then simmered. When it was near sundown the pot was wrapped in straw to insulate it and keep it warm. It would continue to simmer and stay warm until the lunch meal after morning services the next day. In Eastern Europe each family would prepare the cholent at home and bring it to the village bakery, where it was cooked over a slow fire that was lit before the Sabbath began.

The name *cholent* comes from *chaud,* which in French means "warm." The value of a dish which could be kept cooking for a long time not only was good for keeping the Sabbath, but also helped make the food of the poor tasty. The meat used in the cholent was often an inexpensive and tough piece of beef. If it were cooked for just a few hours, you'd need superstrong teeth to chew it. But when it had cooked for a day, it became soft and delicious with the herbs and vegetable flavors it absorbed. Cholent is also a popular Shabbat food because it can be made early on Friday and can be forgotten about until the next day. Today, cholent can be made traditionally, to cook for twenty-four hours, or it can be cooked at a higher temperature and served for Friday-night dinner.

CHOLENT

4–5 pounds brisket of beef
3 cups dried lima beans
2 onions, chopped
4 carrots, cut in half
2 tablespoons rendered chicken fat
12 small red potatoes
2 teaspoons salt
½ teaspoon pepper
¼ teaspoon cinnamon
¼ teaspoon ginger
1 tablespoon paprika
3 tablespoons flour

Soak the lima beans in water overnight. Drain the beans in a colander. Put the meat, onions, carrots, and chicken fat into a large pot (eight-quart size or a dutch oven), and brown the brisket. Turn the meat on all sides until every side is brown. This seals in the meat's juices. Add the salt, pepper, cinnamon, ginger, lima beans, and potatoes. Sprinkle with paprika and flour. Add an inch of water to the pot and cover. After getting an adult's permission, put the pot in a 250° F. oven and bake at least overnight. If this is to be for Friday night, add another inch of water and put the pot in a 350° F. oven for five hours. This recipe will feed 8–10 people.

HUMMUS

Making something on Shabbat that is a treat in Israel is a way of bringing Jerusalem close to home. Hummus is a delicious easy cold dish that makes a good sandwich, a snack between meals, or a first course to a Shabbat dinner.

*2 16 oz.-cans chick peas (also called garbanzo
   beans)*
2 garlic cloves, peeled
1 tablespoon olive oil
juice of one large lemon
pinch of pepper
pinch of salt

Drain the chick peas and put them in a blender. Add the other ingredients and blend until everything becomes a paste. Serve it with pita (flat pocket bread) or matzah.

FRUIT KUGEL

The following recipe is very handy, because it is good as part of the meal or as a dessert, and can be served hot or cold.

3 matzahs
3 egg whites
1 teaspoon vanilla
¼ cup frozen apple juice concentrate
2 large apples, coarsely grated, with skin
1 banana, peeled and sliced
¼ cup raisins
1 orange, peeled and chopped, including juice
1 lemon, peeled and chopped, including juice
½ cup crushed pineapple (canned is all right)

Soak the matzahs in water and drain them. Beat the egg whites with an egg beater until they are stiff. Mix together all the ingredients except the egg whites. Then gently mix in the egg whites so that the whole mixture becomes fluffy. Put the ingredients into a greased 9 × 9-inch baking pan. Bake in a preheated 350° F. oven for one hour. Serve the kugel warm or cold. If the meal is not meat, top it off with a blob of whipped cream for a splendid dessert. (Many Jews observe *kashrut* and do not eat milk and meat together at the same meal.)

Have a terrific Shabbat, but a word of caution: These recipes call for cutting, boiling, and baking. Be sure to have an adult present while you're cooking.

7
CRAFTS

*How many are the things You have made,
O Lord; You have made them all with
wisdom; the earth is full of Your Crea-
tions.*

PSALMS 104:24

Knowing about Shabbat is one thing, but experiencing it is another. One of the best ways to experience it is to make something to help celebrate the day. Not only will you have the satisfaction of your work, but you'll also be a partner in making Shabbat more beautiful.

The first craft described here is the pushke, the container for tzedakah, giving to those in need. Before Shabbat can begin, the poor must be remembered and cared for. A pushke can be made from anything, but metal containers seem to be traditional. Maybe it's because of the pleasing jingle the coins make when they fall into the can.

PUSHKE

You will need one metal Band-Aid container, a perma-
nent-ink marker pen, a screwdriver, a hammer, a piece
of fine sandpaper, a can of gold spray paint, blue self-
adhesive paper (such as Con-Tact paper), and a pair of
scissors.

Draw a line one and one-half inches long across the
top (the lid) of the container with the marking pen. Po-
sition the screwdriver with the blade on the line. Moving the screwdriver from one end of the line to the
other, hammer down lightly until it penetrates the
metal. This will make the slot for inserting money. (It
must be large enough for both coins and folded bills.)
Open the lid and gently hammer flat the inside jagged
edges of the slot. If they are still rough after hammering,
cover them with cloth tape.

Sand the outside of the container to prepare it for
spray-painting. Take the can outside or, if you must

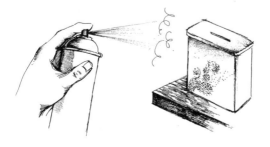

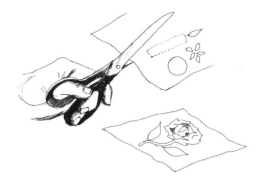

work inside, be sure that you're in a room with an open window. Cover your work area with newspaper, shake the can of spray paint for at least a minute, and spray the container from at least twelve inches away.

While the container dries, prepare designs for the pushke with the adhesive paper. Write PUSHKE on it, or *tzedakah* in Hebrew:

צדקה

Make a few circles traced from coins, or create any Shabbat design you like. Draw the designs and write the letters on the nonsticky side of the adhesive paper. Then cut them out, peel off the paper, and stick them on the coin box.

Every Friday night add a coin or two to the box. It can be either the family pushke or yours alone for your own tzedakah. When it's full, you can take it to a synagogue, where the money will be given to people who need it.

CANDLES

Candles are fun to make for Shabbat, but remember that you must have new ones for each week.

Go to a craft or hobby store (sometimes hardware stores carry craft supplies) and buy two long candle wicks and a box of paraffin. If you want to make colored candles, also buy dye to add to the wax.

Take a large pot, at least the eight-quart size, and fill it with four inches of water. Place it over medium heat on the stove. Then put two empty coffee cans (one-pound size) in the water. Put a block of paraffin in each can. If you want colored candles, add the dye once the wax melts. Try using a different color for each can.

Tie the wicks onto a stick or pencil, far enough apart from one another so that they can be dipped into both cans at the same time. Each time you dip the wicks, the

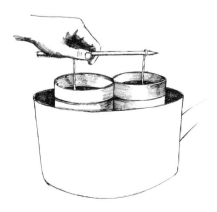

wax will harden around it. If you reverse the direction of the pencil for each dipping, you will get alternating colors in each candle. For example, if you want red and blue, after the first dip you will have one very skinny red wick and one skinny blue wick. Turn the pencil around, and then the blue candle will go into the red wax and the red candle will go into the blue wax. Keep dipping until the candles are three-quarters inch thick. Let the candles dry, still attached to the pencil, overnight. This thickness will burn long enough for Shabbat dinner. Untie them the next day, and the wick for lighting will be the part that was tied to the pencil. You can save the coffee cans if they still have enough wax for more candles.

The alternating colors will give the finished candle an unusual color, and it will melt in different colors. Because hot wax is difficult to handle, this is a good project to do with an adult.

HAVDALAH CANDLE

A Havdalah candle has the advantage of lasting for many Sabbaths, because it's lit only for the short Havdalah ceremony. You can make your own, using the same method as for Shabbat candles. But instead of making two candles, make three very thin candles, no more than one-quarter inch thick. While the candles are soft, braid them. Or you can buy three very thin candles, put them in a 200° F. oven for five minutes, take them out, and braid them. You can either have all the candles the same color, or mix the colors to make a rainbow Havdalah candle.

CANDLESTICKS

Here is a simple way to make candlesticks that will last for years. You will need four flat stones, two screw-on bottles caps, white or epoxy glue, and spray paint.

Find four flat stones that can be easily stacked on top of one another. Figure out which two will look best together. Then divide the stones into two pairs. Take the two bottle caps and place them on top of a pair of stones. Glue to hold with white glue, or use an epoxy glue if you want to wash the wax off the candlesticks later without their coming apart.

Let the glue dry for an hour. Then, holding the spray can twelve inches away, spray the candlesticks with a metallic color or any color that appeals to you. If you have paint left over from the pushke, you can use that.

A variation of this is to find two large flat seashells, like clam shells. Spray-paint two bottle caps and glue one inside each shell. There is no need to paint these candlesticks, because the lovely natural color of the shell will be enough.

SPICE BOX

Many besamim boxes take the form of little houses or castles. You can make your own with two empty raisin boxes. You will also need three different colors of self-adhesive paper, a manila folder or construction paper, liquid white glue, a pair of scissors, and a straight pin. Glue the boxes together, back to back. Cover the sides, but not the bottom or top, with adhesive paper. Cut out windows and a door on a contrasting color of adhesive paper and stick them onto the sides. You can make your little house a cottage or an apartment building, depending upon how many and what size windows you choose. Make the roof by cutting out four triangles from the manila folder or construction paper. Measure the bottom edges of the triangles to fit the sides of the roof before you start cutting. Tape the four pieces together to make a roof. Tape the roof to the house, and cover with the last color of adhesive paper. Punch at least twenty holes in the house with a straight pin. Open the flaps on the bottom to insert sweet spices, such as whole cloves and pieces of cinnamon bark.

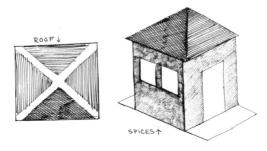

8

ShABBAT FUN

Call the Sabbath a delight.

ISAIAH 58:13

Here are some puzzles and word games to keep you busy on Shabbat without making you work. Since you're not supposed to write on Shabbat, all the puzzles and word games in this chapter can be figured out without paper and pencil.

WORD EQUATIONS

Figure out the missing words to make each "equation" complete. For example, 7 = D. of the W. translates into 7 = Days of the Week. All the equations have to do with Shabbat or the Jewish holidays.

5 = B. of M. 39 = F.A. of S.

13 = Y.O. for a B.M. 8 = N. of H.

3 = P.: A., I., and J. 2 = H. for S.

30 = D. of the L.C. 40 = D. and N. of the F.

4 = M.: S., R., L., and R. 1 = G. Who C. the W.

STINKY PINKY

A stinky pinky is a word riddle. The answer must consist of an adjective and a noun of two syllables that rhyme. For example: What is a wrecker of light? A candle vandal. If the two words of the answer have only one syllable each, the answer is called a "stink pink."

What is a stink pink for cinnamon?
A stinky pinky for a homework partner?
A stink pink for war?
A stinky pinky for a Shabbat floral bouquet?
A stink pink for Shabbat?

RHYMES

Here are words that rhyme with many other words. Sit down with a friend and see how many you can find.

Wine
Bread
Peace
Rest
Time

WORD SEARCH

In each sentence below, a word related to Shabbat is hidden. Can you find it?

1. Bob raided the refrigerator when he arrived home from school.
2. She tried to win every contest.
3. Max found the hall a horrible mess.
4. Ivan's even temper won him friends.

ANSWERS

WORD EQUATIONS

 5 Books of Moses
13 Years Old for a Bar or Bat Mitzvah
 3 Patriarchs: Abraham, Isaac, and Jacob
30 Days of the Lunar Cycle
 4 Matriarchs: Sarah, Rebecca, Leah, and Rachel
39 Forbidden Acts of Shabbat
 8 Nights of Hanukkah
 2 Hallot for Shabbat
40 Days and Nights of the Flood
 1 God Who Created the World

STINKY PINKY

nice spice
study buddy
cease peace
flower power
best rest

RHYMES

Wine

brine	fine	shrine	thine
confine	line	sign	twine
decline	mine	spine	vine
define	nine	stein	whine
dine	pine	sunshine	
divine	shine	swine	

Bread

bed	fled	red	thread
bled	head	said	tread
bred	instead	shed	wed
dead	lead	shred	
dread	led	sled	
fed	read	spread	

Peace

cease	geese	lease	police
crease	grease	niece	release
fleece	increase	piece	

Rest

best	guest	protest	west
blessed	jest	quest	wrest
breast	lest	stressed	zest
crest	nest	suggest	
dressed	pest	test	
guessed	pressed	vest	

Time

chime	dime	lime	rhyme
climb	grime	mime	slime
clime	I'm	prime	thyme
crime			

WORD SEARCH

1. *braided:* Bo*b raided* the refrigerator when he got home from school.
2. *wine:* She tried to *win e*very contest.
3. *hallah:* Max found the *hall a h*orrible mess.
4. *seven:* Ivan'*s even* temper won him friends.

AFTERWORD

The worst of the impulses is to forget one's royal descent.

RABBI SOLOMON OF KARLIN

What makes Shabbat so important is not simply that it celebrates the creation of the world but that it also celebrates creativity in the human being. In other words, Shabbat is not only observed in memory of something that once happened. It recognizes a creative force that continues every day. People don't stop growing, learning, and changing when they reach physical maturity. This process goes on as long as they live.

For people who have difficulty imagining God, the creation story offers a clue. A person's creativity is holy. It isn't only artists who are creative. Every choice a person makes in his or her life is a creative act. Just as God said that His creation was very good, people can look at their lives on Shabbat and say their creation is very good, too.

Appendix

THE 39 FORBIDDEN ACTS OF THE SABBATH

Plowing
Sowing
Reaping
Sheaf-making
Threshing
Winnowing
Selecting
Sifting
Grinding
Kneading
Baking
Sheep-shearing
Bleaching
Combing raw material
Dyeing
Spinning
Inserting thread into a loom
Weaving
Removing the finished
   article

Separating into threads
Tying a knot
Untying a knot
Sewing
Tearing
Trapping
Slaughtering
Skinning or flaying
Tanning
Scraping
Marking out
Cutting to shape
Writing
Erasing
Building
Demolishing
Kindling a fire
Extinguishing a fire
The final hammer blow
Carrying in a public place

GLOSSARY

AMIDAH—The Hebrew word for "standing"; a key prayer recited during synagogue services.

ARK—A covered floating vessel which Noah built for protection against the Flood.

ARON HA-KODESH—The wooden chest in which the Torah is kept; the Hebrew words for "holy ark."

BAR MITZVAH—The Hebrew words for "son of the commandment"; a ceremony held when a Jewish boy reaches the age of thirteen.

BAT MITZVAH—The Hebrew words for "daughter of the commandment"; a ceremony held when a Jewish girl reaches the age of twelve and a half or thirteen.

BERCHES—German bread.

BERCHTA—A German goddess of vegetation.

BERESHIT—The first book of the five books of the Torah, it is also called Genesis.

BESAMIM—The spices used in the Havdalah ceremony.

BIMAH—A raised platform where the Torah is read.

BIRKHAT HA-BANIM—A blessing for parents to say to their children.

BIRKHAT HA-HODESH—A special blessing said on the Sabbath that precedes the new moon.

BIRKHAT HA-LEVANAH—A blessing of the new moon.

BIRKHAT HA-MAZON—A blessing said after a meal.

CANTOR—A person who leads a congregation in prayer and song.

CHAI—The Hebrew word for "life"; its numerical equivalent is eighteen.

C.E.—Common Era. Christians use the term A.D. (Anno Domini, which means "in the year of the Lord").

CHOLENT—A traditional hot meal eaten for Shabbat lunch.

ELIJAH—A prophet of ancient Israel who helped the poor; it is said in the Bible that he will return to announce the Messiah's coming.

ERUV—The Hebrew word for "fence"; the restriction of moving things on Shabbat can be lifted if objects are moved inside the boundaries of a fence.

EXODUS—The second book of the five books of the Torah; the ancient Jews' departure from Egypt to escape slavery.

GEFULTE—The Yiddish word for "stuffed"; gefulte fish is a Shabbat treat.

GENESIS—The first book of the five books of the Torah; it is also called Bereshit.

HAFTARAH—A section from the Prophets, read after the Torah portion, that is in some way connected to the Torah reading.

HALLAH (hallot, pl.)—An egg bread eaten on Shabbat and other Jewish festivals.

HA-MOTZI—A prayer said over hallah before a meal.

HANUKKAH—The eight-day winter holiday or Feast of Dedication celebrated by lighting one candle each night.

HAVDALAH—A ceremony that ends Shabbat; it's the Hebrew word for "separation."

HIGH HOLY DAYS—Rosh Hashanah and Yom Kippur, the most important Jewish holidays of the year.

KABBALAT SHABBAT—The psalms and "Lekhah Dodi" that are sung at the beginning of Friday-night synagogue services.

KABBALIST—A person who believes in special, mysterious religious meanings that go beyond external rituals.

KALLEH—A bride.

KASHRUT—The dietary laws of Judaism.

KIDDUSH—A Friday-night prayer said at home over a glass of wine to proclaim the holiness of Shabbat; it is the Hebrew word for "sanctification."

KIPPAH—A head covering worn out of respect for God.

"LEKHAH DODI"—The Kabbalat Shabbat song which begins "Come, my love, to greet the Sabbath Bride."

MANNA—A special food that God gave the Jews when they were in the desert for forty years.

MARRANOS—Spanish Jews of the fifteenth century who were forced to become Christians but who practiced Judaism secretly.

MELAVVEH MALKAH—A special meal eaten on Saturday night to say farewell to the Shabbat Queen; the Hebrew words for "escorting the queen."

MENUHAH—Shabbat rest.

MIDRASH—A legend or tale that explains a part of the Torah.

MIKVEH—A special bath in which prayers of purification are said; the bath symbolizes a washing away of the week's busyness.

MITZVAH (mitzvot, pl.)—A good deed; a rule or commandment that Jews believe was given to them by God for leading a good life.

MOUNT MORIAH—The highest point in Israel and the place where the new moon was spotted each month.

NESHAMAH YETERAH—An extra soul said to be given to a person to help him or her experience the extraordinary joy of Shabbat.

NISAN—The Hebrew month in which Passover falls.

ONEG SHABBAT—The "Delight of the Sabbath"; a snack of tea and cake after Friday-night and Saturday-morning services.

PASSOVER—A spring holiday that celebrates freedom. It is observed at home with family and friends.

PURIM—The merriest holiday of the year; puppet shows and dancing are part of the celebration.

PUSHKE—A container in which money is put for the poor; this is usually done before the candles are lit on Shabbat.

ROSH HASHANAH—The beginning of the Jewish year; it is part of the High Holy Days.

ROSH HODESH—The monthly holiday of the new moon.

SAFED—A city in Israel where Kabbalists lived.

SAMBATYON—A mythical river which flowed six days and rested on the seventh. It offered protection to the Jewish people.

SAPATTU—A Babylonian holiday that may have influenced the customs of the Jewish Sabbath.

SE'UDAH SHELISHIT—The third Sabbath meal.

SHABBAT BERESHIT—The Shabbat after Simhat Torah when the first portion of the Torah, Bereshit, is read.

SHABBAT HA-GADOL—The Sabbath before Passover; the Great Sabbath.

SHABBAT HA-HODESH—The Sabbath on which Nisan is marked as the first Hebrew month of the year and the laws of Passover are described.

SHABBAT HA-MALKAH—The Sabbath Queen.

SHABBAT HAZON—The Sabbath before Tishah be-Av.

SHABBAT MEVAREKHIM—The Shabbat before each new moon.

SHABBAT NAHAMU—The Shabbat after Tishah be-Av.

SHABBAT PARAH—The Shabbat that falls two weeks before the month of Nisan.

SHABBAT ROSH HODESH—Any Shabbat which coincides with the occurrence of the new moon.

SHABBAT SHEKALIM—The Shabbat before the Hebrew month of
Adar when the Torah portion describes paying some money to
the Temple for its upkeep.

SHABBAT SHIRAH—The Shabbat when the song of Moses is part of
the Torah portion.

SHABBAT SHUVAH—The Shabbat before Rosh Hashanah.

SHABBAT ZAKHOR—The Shabbat of Remembrance, which falls before Purim.

SHABBOS—The Yiddish word for Shabbat.

SHALOM ALEICHEM—Hebrew words for "peace be with you."

SHAMMAI—A teacher in the first century C.E.

SHAVUOT—A spring harvest holiday that celebrates the giving of
the Torah by God to Moses.

SHEKEL (shekels or shekalim, pl.)—Money in ancient Israel.

SHOFAR—A ram's horn that was blown to announce important
events such as Shabbat. Today, it's blown only on the High Holy
Days.

SIMHAT TORAH—"Rejoicing of the Torah"; the holiday celebrating the completion of the Torah reading and the beginning of
the new readings.

SOFER—A scribe who carefully writes the letters of the Torah; it
takes two years to complete a Torah.

SUKKOT—The fall harvest festival celebrated in a little leafy
house.

TALLIT (tallitot, pl.)—A prayer shawl.

TALMUD—Commentaries written about the Torah 1,500 years
ago.

TISHAH BE-AV—The saddest holiday of the year; it recalls the destruction of the Temple.

TZEDAKAH—The act of giving to those in need; justice.

TZITZIT—The fringes on the edge of a tallit.

ZEMIROT (zemirah, sing.)—The songs sung at the Shabbat table.

SUGGESTED READING

Central Conference of Reform Rabbis. *A Shabbat Manual.* New York: Ktav, 1972.

Miriam Chaikin. *The Seventh Day.* New York: Doubleday, 1980.

Theodore Gaster. *Festivals of the Year.* New York: William Morrow & Co., 1972.

Dayan I. Grunfeld. *The Sabbath: A Guide to Its Understanding and Observance.* Jerusalem: Feldheim Publishers, 1959.

Abraham Joshua Heschel. *The Sabbath: Its Meaning for Modern Man.* New York: Farrar, Straus, and Giroux, Inc., 1975.

Abraham E. Millgram. *Sabbath: The Day of Delight.* Philadelphia: Jewish Publication Society of America, 1959.

Hayyim Schauss. *The Jewish Festivals.* New York: Schocken Books, 1978.

Richard Siegal. *The First Jewish Catalog.* Philadelphia: Jewish Publication Society of America, 1973.

Michael Strassfeld. *A Shabbat Haggadah: For Celebration and Study.* New York: Institute of Human Relations Press, 1981.

INDEX